HEBREW
WORD STUDY

A Hebrew Teacher's Call to Silence

CHAIM BENTORAH

ISBN: 978-1-4907-1540-7 (sc)
ISBN: 978-1-4907-1539-1 (e)

Trafford rev. 09/24/2013

 www.trafford.com

North America & international
toll-free: 1 888 232 4444 (USA & Canada)
fax: 812 355 4082

BE STILL AND KNOW THAT I AM

GOD

Psalms 46:11

TABLE OF CONTENTS

Introduction

I am sitting in the meditation room at the Abbey facing an empty chair. I have been doing this every day while fulfilling God's call on my life to spend a week in silence. Paul tells us that faith is the substance of things hoped for and the evidence of things not seen (Hebrew 11:1). The word for hope in the Aramaic is a positive imagination. Paul, being the good Semite might have had that word in mind when he wrote this verse. Faith is the substance of your positive imagination and the evidence of things not seen. For me the most positive thing I can imagine is Jesus and He just happens to be someone that I cannot see. Therefore, every day in my call to silence I have been coming to this meditation room facing an empty chair and imagining Jesus sitting in that chair across from me and by faith we are having a conversation.

I have been telling him how foolish I was on my first day of silence. I was filled with all sorts of expectations. I expected to see miracles, visions, portals opening to heaven or maybe an Apostle Paul like trip to the third heavens. Perhaps I would even get a glimpse of some future event. I mean, here I was sacrificing a week of my busy schedule so I could travel hundreds of miles to a place so desolate that I could not even get a signal on my cell phone, let alone being able to activate my hot spot for the internet. I came down here to this monastery to spend a week in silence. Now you would think that would be good for at least an angelic visit to give me some direction in my ministry. I was even foolish enough to ask God for my ministry to go in a specific direction that I so desired. Well, that all seems so mundane now after my week of silence.

What God did reveal to me was my heart's desire. The thing is I just did not realize my heart's desire when I first arrived at the Abbey. I thought I knew, but in silence I discovered I really did not understand my own heart. Christians take Psalms 37:4: "Delight, thyself in the Lord and He will give you the desires of your heart" quite literally. They spend a lot of time trying to delight themselves in the Lord hoping that if they get enough *delight* God will see fit to grant their heart's desire which they believe to be a healing, a financial miracle, or a restored marriage. Yet, until the veil is ripped from our hearts, do we actually know and understand what our real heart's desire is. Some find that veil ripped from their hearts through a season of prayer, Bible study or fasting. For me it was silence.

In silence my heart saw what my eyes could not see, my heart heard what my ears could not hear and my heart spoke what my lips could not speak. In silence I was able to enter a special room in God's heart, a quiet room, a weeping room. In this room I found Jesus holding a heart in His hands, a heart which had been broken. He was weeping over that broken heart. He was feeling the heart's hurt and loneliness. He wept over that wounded heart longing so much to heal the wound that tore it apart, but the heart's owner would not seek his comfort. I saw Him pick up a heart that was cold and barren and watched his tear drops just roll off that heart. I could sense Him wishing that each tear would somehow penetrate that heart, but the heart's owner would not open it to Him to allow His tears to enter and soften his heart. As He picked up another broken heart I reached out to Him and touched His nail pierced hand and instantly I felt His sorrow and pain, the anguish felt by the heart's owner and I too wept. All three of us wept. It was in this quiet, weeping room that I saw my own heart's desire. It was to not have a flourishing ministry, books published, or to even experience a healing of my body, it was only to seek and search for these heart's owners and let them know that there is a Savior weeping for them, longing to enter their wounded heart to allow His tears, His nailed pierced hands heal those wounds.

I kept a journal of my journey into silence as writing a journal is my way of meditation. As a Hebrew teacher I was able to peer into the very depths and soul of each word that Jesus shared with me from Scripture. As my journey into silence progressed, so did the depth of my understanding of each word.

I cannot share my entire journal with you as many of the things I experienced were just too personal and meant only for my heart and God's alone. However, as I did promise to share some of my journal with you, I will share those portions that I feel open and led to share.

May you be encouraged to spend time in silence, for it is in silence that you will hear the world's weeping and God weeping for them.

CHAPTER I

Rest

IT IS MY FIRST day in silence and I am sitting outside the chapel overlooking a beautiful pasture and watching a mourning dove flutter across the ground. I just opened my Hebrew Bible like some mystic and pointed my finger to the first verse I come to. It is Isaiah 66:1: "Where is my resting place." Hebrew for resting is *mauchah* which means to be quiet, silent. I haven't read this verse in its context yet, but I sense God is trying to start me off on the right foot here. I need to find Gods silent or quiet place, His place to rest in silence.

I think about this. Perhaps God has called me to silence because he wants to spend some time in silence, resting in this silence with me. Yes, even my search for silence has become a selfish thing, my seeking, my longings, my desires. Yet, what is God desiring, why would God seek silence? I am realizing that if I get a revelation from God here, there would be no one to share it with. I cannot access the internet and although I am not a prisoner and I can leave the compound at any time, that would seem to violate God's call upon me. Now if I get a revelation or insight, it is for me and me alone.

Checking this verse further I find the words *ah zen* to be in a construct form. Odd, but both words mean *where, how, when, behold* or *who?* Judging from the context and the following verse it would appear a proper rendering would be: *who is my silence or who is the one I can find in silence or stillness.* The answer is found in verse 2, it is the one who is poor and of a contrite spirit. The word *poor is 'ane* which means one who is depressed in mind or circumstances. Indeed my circumstances are very depressing right now. It is also one with a contrite spirit. The word contrite in Hebrew is *nakah* which means a dejected spirited. I claim that part of the verse also.

So I come to this place of silence with depressed circumstances and a dejected spirit and it is here that God will find His rest. I think I understand. I barely walked into this place of silence and I began to weep. The word *weep* is *baki* which has a numerical value of 32. The word for heart is *lav* which has a numerical value of 32. The sages teach that weeping comes from the heart. My heart weeps for I know that my pride, my unclean thoughts, and my attitudes have wounded *His heart.* Yet, by allowing my heart to weep I am allowing God to reach into my heart, forgive the wounds I brought to His heart and it is here that He finds His rest.

CHAPTER 2

Weeping

I HAVE WEPT THROUGH my repentance, but still I weep. I know now it is not I who weeps but God who is weeping as I join my heart with Him. I feel His pain and sorrow for those who have a broken His heart. But Gods heart also weeps for the pain and suffering of this world. I fear, to be honest, I have not risen to this level of weeping. Perhaps in my time of silence I shall rise to that level. Perhaps in silence I will hear the cry of this world with the ears of my heart, I shall see the suffering of this world with the eyes of my heart, and maybe, maybe God will allow me to speak to the suffering with the lips of my heart. Dear precious Father God, my dearest Friend, Companion and Counselor, please let it be so.

I am enjoying my first meal here at the Abby in silence. I just read Isaiah 66:6 which says "Hark, an uproar from the city," when someone broke the rule of silence. He only spoke quietly and that was to ask a brother a question. However, in the silence of the room all heads turned and it was like a booming voice or an uproar. The word for *uproar* is *sha'on* which is a crashing sound like a wave hitting the rocks on a shore. In context of this verse, that *uproar* is a noise from the temple, it is a sound that does not belong there. It is as if the Lord is reminding me that for this week in silence, I must beware of any *uproar* or *sha'on* anything that does not belong in this time of silence. I must not let the voice of my health concerns, ministry concerns, financial concerns or any voice intrude in this time that God and I have together. This is His time, not my health concern times, my ministry concern time, or my financial concern times. God cannot find His rest in me or I in Him if these voices intrude.

CHAPTER 3

Correction

WHAT A STRANGE ENVIRONMENT this Abbey is. You have no social obligations or duties. There is no phone, no internet, and no communication whatsoever. You are not required to attend mass, daily prayers or join the brothers in their chants if you do not desire. No one is watching you, no one says "hi" or even acknowledges your presence. When your time is up you drop your key in the little box and leave. There is no one to say goodbye to nor any bill to settle up. There is only one Person you are here to speak with, there is only one Friend to make or renew a friendship with.

It is now 3:00 in the afternoon. I am tempted to look for a schedule to find out who the speaker is tonight, or what workshops are available. But, of course, there are no speakers, teachers or workshop leaders. Ok, I stand corrected, there is one guest Speaker, just one workshop Leader and He is speaking 24/7.

I have been on many retreats and attended many conferences, I have heard some of the best speakers, teachers and preachers at these retreats, but this is the first retreat where God Himself is the keynote (and only) speaker.

Hold it, I take that back, there is a guest speaker right now. He has just flown to a tree right in front of me. He is looking right at me and now he is speaking: "Chirp, chirp!" Oh, sorry, you have to listen with your heart. He is saying: "Turn with me to Isaiah 1:18." All of sudden he flies from the tree right toward me. I duck, it was that close, like he wanted to make sure he had my attention. I look back at the tree, it is a massively large tree and unlike all the other trees it is white, pure white. At first I thought the tree was dead, but then I notice it had leaves, very light colored green leaves. This guest speaker was a black bird and although the tree is massive, you could not help but see that little black speck on the tree.

Rev. Black Bird was teaching me about Isaiah 1:18: "Come now and let us reason together:" The word reason in Hebrew is *yakach* which really means to correct, to bring into right order, to bring into harmony or to be in tune. Rev. Black Bird was not in harmony with that tree, he was totally out of tune as the tree was an entirely different color. A white dove would be in harmony with that totally white tree, but of course Rev. Black Bird was not a dove and that was his sermon to me, I was totally out of harmony with the purity of God.

What is God saying in Isaiah 1:18? He is saying: "Come let us get corrected." Yes, it is in a cohortative form and He is asking me to join Him in a correcting process where I can be in harmony with Him. But, like Rev. Black Bird I cannot become a dove. The only way Rev. Black Bird can become the same color as the tree is if I splashed a bucket of white paint on him. Although he might fool some of the brothers around here, I would not be fooled, he would not be fooled, nor would the tree be fooled, underneath he would still be a Black Bird and that white coating would soon wear off. No, the only way to become a dove is to be born a dove, he has to be born again.

"Lord, I renew that prayer I made fifty years ago to be born again. Come, let us be united together, and make a correction. Though my sins be as scarlet, make them white as snow, like this tree made of the same material upon which you died." White in Hebrew is shalag. In other words God will take all my sins, mistakes, failures and make them white. Shalag is spelled Shin (God's passionate love). God will take all my sins and cover them with his passionate love, and use the next letter, a Lamed which means teaching, he will teach me and instruct me in the ways of His final letter in the word for white which is the Gimmel or His lovingkindness.

As confirmation, one of the retreat members just walked by my white tree. He was dressed all in white, he even had white hair and he blended right in with that white tree. He paused in front of that tree long enough to—where did he go? Funny, he just seemed to disappear like—Oh my gosh! I haven't even been here one day and already I'm seeing things. Don't tell my study partner, she will say it was a vision. Still, I feel God is confirming that I am no longer a Black Bird on a White Tree. Because of the sacrifice of Jesus on that tree 2,000 years ago, I am truly as white as snow and in harmony with Him.

CHAPTER 4

Purge

CHECKED OUT THE ABBEY's library, not much there, but then this is a monastery and not a university. There seems to be a lot of books on grief, dealing with illnesses, tragedies and life's many stresses. I never stopped to consider, but I assume some people come here to seek solitude in order to confront some tragedy in their life and not so much to seek the heart of God. Still I see a number of priests who come here just to refresh their relationship with God.

Isaiah 1:25 teaches us that God will purge away our dross with lye. The word in Hebrew for purge is *tearaph* which is really the word for smelting or refining. The word is usually used with refining fires, yet God is saying He will do it with lye. Lye is the closest thing the ancients had to soap. People knew nothing of microbes in those days so they had no need to wash their hands unless they were to touch something sacred. The ground was cursed so the ceremony of hand washing was done to remove anything that was cursed. Water was enough but sometimes you needed something a little stronger to really get the grit out, so lye was used.

Although lye is pretty harsh to us, it was not so bad to the ancients who did not have the luxury of Ivory Soap or Irish Spring. At least the cleansing of lye was not as rough as the refining fires or the harsh acid chemicals used to refine silver. Although God sometimes uses the tragedies in our lives to draw us closer to Him, there are harsher methods He could employ. I suspect those who seek silence to lick their wounds end up with a little bonus at the end of their retreat, they find a gentle cleansing of earthly passions in the lovingkindness of God.

CHAPTER 5

Mighty Tree

I AM BEGINNING TO think the Abbey is built on a cemetery. I guess when the brothers complete this life's journey they are buried right on the grounds of the monastery. With the Abbey being 150 years old, that can add up to a lot of grave sites. This seems to be a constant reminder that our journey through this life is but a short one. We are just passing through, enjoying a few sights but our real destination is somewhere beyond the blue.

Isaiah 1:29: "For you shall be as a terebinth whose leaf fades. The word in Hebrew for terebinth is 'ayil which means a mighty tree. All that this tree produces while it is alive dies in just a few short months, no matter how mighty the tree is. So what about all the leaves we produce in our lifetime, all our accomplishments and achievements? When that little white cross with our name on it pops up out of the ground, what will all our fancied greatness be worth? As the old song we sang in Sunday School goes: "Only one life to offer, Only one life that soon will pass, only what's done for Christ will last."

CHAPTER 6

Tremble

SUNDAY MORNING ON MY way to the Monastery, I stopped off to worship with a congregation in Indiana. The leader of this congregation quoted Isaiah 1:5: "Hear the word of the Lord, ye that tremble at his word." This man of God said that he was so moved by the previous service that he trembled. When you hear the words tremble you think of being so fearful that you are shaking in your boots. I cannot imagine that this person who so loves God would be fearful of God's words. The word in Hebrew for tremble is *charad* which means to shake with great emotion, be it fear, sorrow, or pure joy. This person did not say which emotion caused him to shake, perhaps he does not really know himself.

I am sitting in a prayer room at this moment looking out of a window at the rolling hills of the Kentucky landscape. On the window sill is a small sculpture of Jesus kneeling over the earth. His head is in His arms and He is weeping over the world. The image is so lifelike, I could actually see him *charad (shake)*. I called a little mourning dove to be with me in this moment. He is outside the window right now cooing his mournful coo. In fact he is right in front of the sculpture of Jesus who is weeping as I weep and the little dove is mournfully cooing (this is my second day of silence, you will have to forgive my weirdness). All three of us are expressing our mourning for the suffering of this world. My little dove friend has such a pure heart and is so near to the heart of God that he is drawing me closer to the heart of God to see what He is specifically weeping over. In my heart I can see what my physical eyes do not see. I see Him holding the heart of one particular child that He is weeping over. It is a young teenage girl, about thirteen or fourteen. Her name starts with a *K* and she has a wound so deep that she will not allow her heart to open and release the tears. That shell around *K's* heart is so harden, no one can enter, not even Jesus. I look at Jesus as He holds this hardened heart and as He weeps over it. I reach out and lay my hand on His over this precious little heart. Instantly I begin to weep. I say to Jesus, let me weep for her, let this doves cooing soften this dear heart so that it will break open and release all those tears that have built up inside of it, so that she may cry out all that emotional hurt, pain and sorrow. Then when her heart has emptied of all its tears, you can fill it the joy of your heart.

So as Jesus weeps, I cry and our mourning dove softly coos I speak to this gentle heart. Weep, my little K, weep until there are no more tears and your heart will be filled with the Love of God in Christ Jesus. Dear little

K, I shall likely never meet you in this world, but one day we will meet in the world that is yet to come. When we do I shall tell you of your little dove who flew to my window to lead a chorus of tears from the heart of Jesus and my heart joined with Him and we all wept over your gentle heart that was so broken.

Chapter 7

Give Thanks

It is such a unique feeling to get up in the morning and know I have nothing to do, no obligations, no expectations, the only thing I have to do, the only thing there is do is just be with Jesus and listen to the infinite sounds of His voice. I hear his voice with my physical ears with every song being sung by his birds and the sound of the wind blowing through the leaves. If I listen with my heart I can understand what they are saying. They speak the words of Scripture. "I have loved you with an everlasting love." "His name shall be called Wonderful, Marvelous, Counselor, Prince of Peace, Mighty God, and Everlasting Father."

"Hello little Robin!" Hoo boy, get the net, get the net, I'm talking to robins now. He is saying something right now, I must listen with my heart, "Yea, ok, Psalms 7:18." So I look up Psalms 7:18 and it says that I will give thanks unto the Lord according to His righteousness. That word *give thanks* is one word in Hebrew *yadah*. It is

15

spelled Yod (message from heaven), Daleth (a doorway) to the Hei (God's presence). What *yadah* is telling me is that giving thanks is a doorway to God's presence. But soft, that word *yadah* has a secondary meaning which is confession of sins. Am I still in this sin confessing mode? I look up at my Robin friend and he is just bobbing his head up and down. I notice he is sitting on a dying tree, but he is on one of the few branches that still have some green leaves. It is sort of like Jesus is telling me that even in the midst of death, he will be found on whatever branch still has life. Where He goes, wherever He rest, there is always life for He is life.

When I first sat down I could not see any birds, now they are all around. My attention is drawn to one robin hopping around the ground. He suddenly jumps onto the branch of a dead tree and looks at me. "Yeah, I get it" I say, "I am just a dead tree and my ministry is really just a dead ministry. It is going to go nowhere." The Mr. Robin turns his head toward the tip of the branches and I realize that the tree is not dead, it is just a late bloomer. I see the branches filled with buds that will one day soon blossom into beautiful leaves. All the other trees are in bloom except this one. My robin friend is just pointing out to me that even if it seems like all my former classmates from seminary now have ministries in full bloom it doesn't' mean I have a ministry that is dead, just one that is a late bloomer.

CHAPTER 8

The Calvary Road

I AM TAKING A walk through the woods right now, following a rustic trail that is supposed to lead to some statues. It is not an easy road, at least for one who has a protruding hernia like I do and is not wearing his brace. The trail is filled with hills to climb and narrow bridges to cross. I guess this is supposed to remind us of the road that Jesus took to the cross. I wonder, what those statues will be? Will they be of Jesus or the apostles who also walked a difficult road. Perhaps they will be of some martyred saints who walked a difficult road for Jesus. Well, I will press on to find out.

The brothers set up little shrines along the way so you can stop and pray. For a 62 year old man, it is a nice place to catch a breath and to give my hernia a little break. My hernia is starting to rebel. However, the Roman soldiers did not give Jesus a break when He walked that Calvary road and He had more than a hernia to contend with. So I press on in the fellowship of His suffering in my small symbolic but still rather painful way.

Someone else must have been suffering from a physical affliction while on this journey. They left a little hand written sign with Exodus 20:22: "Thus said the Lord unto Moses: You shall say unto the children of Israel, you yourselves have seen that I have spoken with you from heaven." This old boy must have been convinced God was going to speak to him on his little journey to the statues. My gut is telling me, I hope to hear a message from Him on this journey, because I am beginning to feel the pressure. Although just seeing a portion of Scripture on this journey has a real healing effect on me.

I arrive at a little shack with a sign saying: "Rosary house." There are paper notes tacked all over the wall of this shack posted by other pilgrims. Each reflect someone's soul cry. Some speak words of praise to God: "Jesus you are great" or "I love you Jesus." Some are more of a heart cry: "Heal me, o Lord" "Help me figure myself out" "Help me to forgive." I find myself weeping as I read these little messages to God. Then I spot one that I know is the cry of a true servant of God. "I have known hunger, loneliness and thirst and all was quenched by the Spirit of God, all is well, first things first." Indeed, first things first and that is to find God's heart. So now I continue my journey, just wondering what these statues will portray. I know and understand that I am on this little journey to hear God's heart cry to me. So I walk what I am now certain is a Calvary road. I come to the first statue which has an inscription on it: "May we always remember that the church exist to lead us to Christ in many and varied ways, but it is always the same Christ.—Gethsemane. I look up and I see a sculpture of the disciples who are asleep. I move a little further up the trail to another clearing and there is a large life size statue of Jesus, on His knees, one showing great anguish and agony. It is Jesus in the Garden praying. I hear His heart speak. The church sleeps while Jesus suffers overwhelming agony and grief over a lost world. Can we not stay awake for a little while to the world's cry and to minister to the Master's grieving heart by finding those who he mourns over and sharing His love with them?

It is now time for my return journey. I made it to the statues, I have heard the message Jesus wanted me to hear and I am stricken with grief. I sit down and weep over my callus attitude toward God's broken heart. I then hear a woodpecker tapping on a tree. It is almost like Morse code. Tap, pause, tap, tap—L. Tap, tap, pause—U. Tap, tap, tap Long pause—V. Well maybe not, maybe I am just looking for some message, but LUV does flood me with an overwhelming sense of peace.

Now for the painful journey home. I've read a number of adventures about mountain climbing like Mr. Everest. They all talk of the journey up but say little of the journey down. That, I think, would be the most hazardous part of the journey, you are already exhausted from the long climb up and now you have the same dangers going down. Forget lunch, it will take me twice as long to get down as I will need to take longer breaks to let my hernia catch up with me. It has not been cooperating at all with me today.

CHAPTER 9

Still Waters

To my surprise, I not only made it back in time for lunch, but I also made the entire trip back without feeling any pain from my hernia. Not only that I did not need to stop once to sit down and rest. I was able to use the entire time on my return journey reflecting on what God had just revealed to me about my heart. I suppose I could consider this a miracle, a sign from God or maybe a confirmation that God did indeed speak to me. Perhaps I should just stop speculating and be grateful for His traveling mercies.

I am now having lunch with the brothers, in silence. They allow me to have my I Pad so I can continue with my journal. I reflect how my hike or pilgrimage took me past both running waters and still waters. I wondered why David specifically referenced *still waters* in Psalms 23:2. If I had my choice of drinking water I would take the running water, *still waters* seemed so stagnate. As far as refreshing goes, the flow of the running waters creates coolness in the area giving a refreshing feeling. Still water just sits there and bakes in the hot sun.

The word used in the Hebrew for *still* is *manuchah* which means rest or peace. Yet, there is another possible root word other than *nachan* and that is *manuch* which means *to give as in a sacrifice.* A secondary meaning is that God leads David besides *sacrificial giving waters.* The word for water is *miy* which can be a noun or the interrogative word *who.* I believe David carefully choose his words under the inspiration of God to give us two messages in one. Not only did he say that God leads us beside still waters (to bring us peace) but there is a little play on words here where he is saying: "He leads me to the one who will make a sacrificial gift (which will bring eternal peace).

CHAPTER 10

Clouds

I'm sitting in a screened in porch. The reason I am sitting inside on such a lovely day is that the bugs and I are not in harmony. Besides that this Kentucky sun is brutal. The porch is on a second floor overlooking the compound. As I look straight out I see the hills painted on the backdrop of a blue sky and clouds. I cannot help but think of the old peanuts cartoon where Linus, Lucy and Charlie Brown are looking at the cloud and relating the pictures they see. Linus sees Joshua fighting a fierce battle, Lucy sees Queen Esther being received by the king of Persia. Charlie Brown sees a dog and a cat.

Indeed, we are fascinated with clouds and the various formations that can reveal our inner thoughts as it did with the Peanuts gang. Each saw something different in the same cloud, each eyeing a reflection of their inner thoughts. In fact, the word in Hebrew means just that. No you will not find it in your lexicon or in the back of Strong's. They will simply say the word 'anan means cloud. But the word is spelled Ayin, Nun, Nun. The Ayin speaks to us of Spiritual insight. The Nun is the number fifty. The sages teach that the number fifty represents the fiftieth gate to understanding. The double Nun would show us a complete understanding. In fact two Nuns equal one hundred which is the number of completion according to Jewish literature. Thus, clouds bring us into an understanding of ourselves and our relationship with God. For instance the cloud that I am looking at now looks like a horse galloping. No, I am not thinking of the Kentucky Derby which will create havoc with traffic on I-65 when I head home. Actually, I am thinking of the Hebrew word *soos* which in a noun form means a horse, but comes from the verbal root meaning to be swift or speedy. That old cloud has brought to the surface my real concern. The sand in the hour glass is running out, I have been around this planet for three score and two years and I have accomplished so little for God. If He is going to do anything with my life, He'd better do it now and quickly for this old train is approach the final station.

CHAPTER 11

Create

WELL, JESUS AND I have finally gotten around to having that heart to heart talk. I went to the Meditation Room and there were two chairs facing each other. It was as if two people turned the chairs to face each other to carry on a conversation, which cannot be the case as you are not to carry on any conversations in the Meditation room. The idea is silence after all. So how did the chairs end up facing each other? Either a couple other retreatants were breaking the rules and having a little chat facing each other or someone else is also having a good conversation with Jesus like I was planning to do. You see when I really have one of those down and out conversations with Jesus I will take two chairs and face them to each other and then I will sit in one chair and imagine that Jesus is sitting in the other chain and we have a conversation. This is the first time the chairs naturally face each other, I usually arrange the chairs myself. It is almost like Jesus came ahead of me and rearranged the furniture expecting to have this face to face, heart to heart talk. Of course the idea that He or some angel came a few minutes before my arrival to the Meditation room to set up the chairs is ridiculous, right? I mean really, I'm right am I not? Don't tell my study partner, she will say it was a miracle.

Anyways, we talked, I reflected over the three score and two years of my life and how God has always been faithful to direct my paths. He never once failed. I'm speaking of my life's vocations. Practically every job I had I had prayed for it and God granted it. And now as I approach the final stage of my working, vocational life I have only one more job I want to do. I have made this known to Him. The simple fact is, if he does not grant this one final vocational request, them He will blow a perfect record.

With that out of the way we moved on to the next topic. There are still attitudes of my heart that I have still need to overcome. I told Him I was frustrated, I tried and tried, but I cannot overcome these heart issues. He simply spoke to me Psalms 51:10: "Create in me a clean heart." I took a close look at that word *create* and found it was the word *bara*, the same word used when He created the heavens and the earth. God really did not do that much creating or *bara(ing)*, He only *bara('ed)* the heavens and the earth, the rest he called into being from that which He already created. In fact, the only thing He really is in the business of creating are clean hearts. So like David, I asked Him for a creative miracle, a clean heart.

CHAPTER 12

Inner Most Heart

THIS MORNING I WENT to the meditation room and I wept before Jesus. I don't know why, the tears came from very deep within. I don't know if they were tears of joy, sadness or repentance. I opened my Hebrew Bible and let my finger fall where it may. I have always been warned against this, they called it mysticism. But come now, have we not all, at one time or another followed this little exercise? Believe me I know the joke about the old boy who felt he needed a word from the Lord and blindly opened his Bible, closed his eyes and let his finger fall on verse which happened to be: "And Judas went out and hung himself." Not happy with that he tried again and this time his finger fell on the verse that said: "Go and do thou likewise." Yet, during my time of silence I have been closing my eyes opening my Hebrew Bible and letting my finger fall to a verse. Each time I have been led to a verse which specifically addressed my question or the issue I was dealing with. In my time of silence I seem to be doing this exercise without thinking and not at all being surprised when the verse matches my question or issue.

As I asked Jesus why I was weeping I let my finger fall to a verse which happened to be Psalms 51:8: "Behold, you desire truth in the inward parts, make me therefore to know wisdom in my inner most heart. "My eyes rested on those words *inner most heart.* David is not asking for wisdom in his heart, but his inner most heart, the very core of his heart. As Shakespeare said in Hamlet, "the heart of my heart." I believe the tabernacle and temple were designed to be a picture of one's heart. There was the outer court. In the outer court all are welcomed, even gentiles. That is like the outer layer of our hearts, where we welcome all, lover, friends and strangers alike. Then there was the inner court to the temple, this is where only those who were truly worshippers of God could enter, it is where the priest offered the sacrifices. That is the inner layer of our hearts, the area that we are a little more selective about who gets in, only true lovers, spouses, immediate family are permitted to enter that layer of our hearts. It is where we enter into an intimacy with those special relationships, where we sacrifice for those relationships, and where we share our joy and sorrow. Believers allow Jesus to enter this inner court of their hearts. Yet, there is another area of the temple that is even more selected, it is the area that only one person is allowed to enter, only the high priest, for that is the Holy of Holies, the place where the presence of God resided. Our hearts have a holy of holies, an inner most part, the core of our hearts.

Usually we will allow only one person to enter that chamber of our heart and that would be God.

The word in Hebrew for the *inner most heart is satham*. Oh yes, your lexicon will call it the inner most part, inward parts, etc. But *satham* in its most primitive form means the secret place of your heart. David wants to know *wisdom* in this most secret, private place of his heart. Why wisdom? The word in Hebrew for *wisdom* is *chakam*. The first letter in *chakam* is the Chet. The sages teach us that the Chet is two horizontal lines connected by a vertical line, it is a bridge between two hearts, our hearts and God's heart. The next letter in *chakam* is the Kap which we are told is a vessel, such as our hearts, which need to be filled. In the case of *wisdom or chakam* it needs to be filled with the Final Mem, the last letter to the word *wisdom*. The Final Mem represents the hidden knowledge, the secrets of God. Thus, David is inviting God to share his inner most part of his heart, his holy of holies if God will share the inner most part of His heart, His Holy of Holies, His secrets with him.

In this little meditation room Jesus and I struck a deal, I will share my *satham* the inner core of my heart with Him, if He will share the inner core, His secrets with me. This does come with a price, for if I am to explore the depths of His heart, I must allow Him to explore the secrets of my heart.

CHAPTER 13

An Empty Heart

I AM SITTING IN the balcony of the church sanctuary. It is empty, I am the only one here. The brothers have been here since 3:30 AM praying. They are now off making their cheese, fudge and pottery which they will sell to support the Abbey. Others are tending to the garden where they grow fruits and vegetables which will supplement their diet. Later they will have some free time where they will indulge in their many and varied hobbies like astronomy (there is a small observatory on the compound equipped with a telescope). Some study, some paint, sculpture, and even practice a musical instrument. Yet, all they do they do as unto the Lord, they do in the attitude of prayer, for they practice prayer without ceasing and they do all in silence.

Yet, here in the sanctuary it is empty, clean, spotless, held sacred, yet empty. Jesus has allowed me to enter the heart of His heart and I find it is very lonely in there. Like this sanctuary, few really enter His heart of heart, only on special occasions. A brother just walked in, he is passing through. He pauses long enough to honor the host and then leaves. This is so like many of us Christians, we pop in and out of God's heart pausing long enough to show our respects but never staying around for an extended visit. Yet I look out over this sanctuary and I see the wooden benches, each with its own podium where each brother has his own chair. Some have left their prayer books. Later they will return for their prayers where they will all join their voices in a beautiful chant of praise and worship.

Jesus is reminding me how often we just skim the surface of his heart. A quick "Praise the Lord" or a "Thank you for this food" and we are off gratifying our own desires, wants and need, leaving behind this lover who has prepared a special room for us to stay around and chat, a special meal of the Bread of Life and a chance to feast on His word, but we have to switch on the ball game lest we miss an important play. I can sense the ache in the heart of Jesus: "I have prepared a feast for my loved ones, yet they are too busy with their lives to spend time with me. Did you know that many of my churches actually delayed, shortened and even cancelled their services on Super Bowl Sunday? I prepared this special place for each one, a special feast but they did not want to miss the kick off." Jesus wept. I wept for He was exploring my heart and showed me the many times I was *too busy* to talk with my Lord, my special friend.

I said: "Lord, but there are millions and millions of believers around the world, would I really be missed?" I then thought of an interview I saw on television of a mother of twelve children who had lost one child to gang violence. As she wept the reporter reminder her that she had eleven other children. She responded: "Yes, but it still hurts just as bad as if he were an only child." I thought of the brothers as they gather together for their morning prayers, day after day, month after month, praying together, singing together, chanting together. I listened to their voices during my meditation this morning and they all sang in unison, perfect harmony as they have been doing for years. If just one of those brothers did not show up, he would be missed, the morning prayers would not be the same. Oh, they would go on, but it just would not sound the same. I looked out over the empty sanctuary and realized that this is what God's inner heart is like if I am *too busy* for Him. Oh sure there are others who will enter His inner heart, but like that mother who lost that one child, she may have eleven other children but her house is as empty as that sanctuary with that one child missing. God's inner heart may have many worshipping in it, but if just one of His beloved is missing, that heart is as empty as that sanctuary.

I understand why Jesus led me to this empty sanctuary, He has explored my heart and found that there are other desires, interest, and concerns which are more important than He is. I weep again. How long has it been?

CHAPTER 14

Wilderness

IT IS ABOUT AN hour before lunch. I am lying in my bunk, resting. Yet, I cannot rest. Every moment is important on this retreat. I think of Matthew 4:1: "Then was Jesus led up of the spirit into the wilderness." Jesus spent 40 days in silence. He was *led up of the spirit.* More accurately in the Greek and Aramaic He was led up *by* the spirit. The text does not say what *spirit.* The Aramaic uses the word *roka* which is generally used for an expression of the *Holy Spirit or Spirit of God.* That was His Spirit, for although Jesus had a body and (if we hold to a trichonomist view) soul, His Spirit was the Spirit of God Himself. The Spirit of God dwelled within Jesus. Today that same Spirit dwells within us if we have accepted His gift of salvation. I believe it is this same Spirit that has led me to spend a week at this Abbey in silence.

Jesus was led by the Holy Spirit to the *wilderness.* In the Aramaic this is the word *madbra* which means a desert, or desolate place, a wild, arid region without inhabitants. Well, that is not exactly the place the Holy Spirit has led me but it has a similar effect. I could not have lived in silence at home. Oh sure, I could have taken a week off of work and hung around my apartment, locked myself in, but still there were distractions, there is the internet, TV, shopping areas and any number of things that would take my mind off of my meditations for a few moments or hours. Right now I feel a temptation to hop in my car and go to the town about 15 miles away to purchase a pair of sunglasses, I mean I could really use them here, yet to do that would interrupt a certain flow of the Spirit of God. I don't fully understand it all but I do realize that there is something about spending time in *madbra* where God can have one's undivided attention for a length of time. Even lying in my bunk, having exhausted all my prayers, everything I wanted to say to God, I find that even in that time of rest, the Spirit of God is ministering something to me. The people from the Toronto Blessing call it *soaking*, the ancient Jewish sages call it *devekut* a clinging to God, hugging God and letting Him hug you.

A couple who are married sometimes do not have to say a word to each other, they can run out of things to say, but even in those times, they can still hug each other. You don't need to say a thing in a hug, you just rest in an embrace.

So as I approach the lunch hour, I don't feel like taking a walk, I don't even feel like going outside. I don't feel like praying or even studying the Word of God. I need a break from all of that, but at the same time I do not want to interrupt the flow. Now I could pull up a book from my Kindle on the IPAD, a good novel maybe, or I could just take a nap, nothing wrong with that. Maybe take a shower, maybe I can hook up my earphone to the IPAD and listen to a book on tape, a sermon, a teaching that I have downloaded or just listen to music, nothing wrong with that. But I can do that 51 weeks out of the year. This is God's week, my week in *madbra* where there is a flow of the Spirit of God and I do not want to interrupt it. So what do I do when I have run out of things to do? Maybe the same thing a couple does on their honeymoon or their second honeymoon. After a day of sight-seeing, eating out, walking along a beach holding hands and talking, after a day of all that and they have run out of things to do, then they just settle down and hold each other, not saying a word. Perhaps now it is time that God and I just hold each other, not say a word, just enjoy each other's presence, *soaking* or *devekut*.

CHAPTER 15

Prepare

GOD HAS LED ME to Psalms 78:8 which speaks of a rebellious nation that did not set their hearts aright. Actually, in the Hebrew the word for *set aright* is *kuwn* which means to prepare. In other words they did not prepare their hearts.

The context of this Psalm speaks of Israel during the time of the Exodus when God did some really nifty miracles and yet the people were not satisfied. So every day there was the miracle of manna from heaven and yet the people were not satisfied. They wanted meat, fruits, vegetables and a variety. Surely God wanted them to prosper, should they settle for plan old manna. But just as I am ready to throw rocks at Israel, God shouts out: "Hold it, before you talk of that speck in your brother's eye how about that board in your own eye?"

I suddenly thought of an article I read about the President of a major movie studio, it was either MGM or Paramount. He was a multimillionaire who daily rubbed shoulders with the rich and powerful. He was on location in a third world country and was visiting a garbage dump where children were picking through the trash searching for food or something they could sell. At that moment he received a call on his cell phone from some agent of a famous movie star who was having a melt down because his private jet did not have certain amenities he had ordered. He overheard this movie star in the background screaming and saying that he did not have to live like this. This executive then looked out at these children digging in a garbage dump to find something that would help their families to survive and decided right then and there to resign from his position, move to this third world country and use his wealth to build a school and medical clinic.

I think I am like this movie star, I have so much from God yet I am never satisfied. I keep wanting more. Yes, I am thinking about my conversation with God yesterday concerning my vocation and my request. I am not satisfied with what He has given me, after all He is a rich God, why would He not want to give me the best, why would He not want me to live in comfort and prosperity, I really don't have to live like this, like I am now. Then I hear a little voice inside of me saying: "Have you not learned anything in your time of silence? Have I not shown you My cross and My suffering on that cross?"

I realize that my problem is not one of greed, but it is the same problem that the people of Israel faced, they had not *prepared* (kuwn) their hearts for the miracles that would come. Without a prepared heart, the miracles will only spoil one's soul. Maybe this call to silence is to prepare me for miracles that will follow, if it is, I must prepare my heart so that if and when the miracles come my soul will not be spoiled and be unsatisfied. I will need to learn to accept each miracle from God as possibly the only or last miracle I will receive and be grateful. There is an old story of a servant woman who was washing dishes and praying, thinking she was alone. She prayed: "Oh Lord, if I only had $500 I would be the most satisfied woman in the world." The master of the house overheard this and went in and said he had overheard her prayer and that he would give her the $500. After he left he put his ear to the door to hear her next prayer of thanks to God. However, her next prayer was: "Lord, why didn't you make me say $1,000." I know, some preachers will say I should think big as big as I can and then ask God. If I am learning anything from this time of silence I need not to think big, only to think God.

CHAPTER 16

Quietness

ECCLESIASTES 4:6 "BETTER IS a handful of quietness than both the hands filled with labor and striving after the wind." The Hebrew word for striving is *ra'ah* which is a consuming passion. The word for *better* is *tov* which means to be in harmony with God. The word for quietness is *nachath* which means quietness. The word *nachath* in Hebrew will explain itself. It is spelled Nun, Chet, Taw. The Nun represents productivity which comes from the Chet, a bonding with God and a joining of our hearts with God's heart. This will result in the Taw which speaks of truth and praise resulting in repair and restoration. In quietness we produce more than all our labors could produce in terms of our relationship with God. In fact these labors run the danger of becoming a consuming passion which is like chasing the wind, it will only pass. What is accomplished in quietness is eternal and the product of our quietness is for eternity.

I have seen many ministries which were built on a person and their name. Little effort was made to grow the ministry in quietness, which is to grow it according to the heart of God. It's growth comes from a name recognition. It's leader or followers exalt the name of the founder and tithe to the founder although for the sake of political correctness they say they are tithing to God. The evidence that the ministry was the result of labors filled with a consuming passion for the wind is that after the founder dies, the ministry flounders. Attempts are made to keep the ministry going and many do continue thanks to the hiring of business consultants and business managers who can keep a ministry going just as they can keep any business going. Then there are ministries which do continue and flourish after its founder dies. I was listening on the radio to one such minister who passed away over twenty years ago. He still teaches on recordings and all his teachings are simple teachings on and from the Bible itself. That ministry was one that grew in *quietness (nachath)*. I am praying that my little ministry will be modeled after this one. It will be a simple ministry of the Word of God. It will be built on a desire to know and study the Word of God and my name will not be found anywhere, even in its articles of incorporation.

As I sit back and smugly smile over my pious and humble declaration I sense Jesus is staring back at me. "Jesus, are you not impressed that I want a ministry to be built on *nachath?*" Jesus's only response is, that all ministries were built on *nachath* but once the power, fame and wealth entered another name took over. "Well,"

I say, "On that count, you have nothing to worry about, my ministry will never grow to the point where it will have power, fame and wealth. It will be just a nice little homespun ministry." Jesus's only response was: "That is what concerns me." I think I will have to meditate on that response."

CHAPTER 17

Likeness

Psalms 17:15: "As for me I will behold thy face in righteousness, I will be satisfied to awake in thy likeness." David says he will *behold*. In Hebrew this is the word *chazah* which in its root form means to experience. David will experience God's presence in righteousness. He will experience this presence when He is doing the right thing. I think I am beginning to understand. I have been experiencing God's presence in these days of silence but there are times when my thoughts shift away from God, I begin to pondering other things. I am aware I am not doing what is right because I suddenly no longer feel His presence. As I pondered this idea, I read the rest of the verse. It says that David will be satisfied to awake with God's likeness. The word *likeness* in Hebrew is *temonah* which basically means to be in someones image, not so much a physical image but in His image with our actions and personality. I recently heard a preacher who was a guest speaker at a congregation. He was very much

41

a *temonah*. This was apparent in the way comb his hair and the way he preached with a lot of shouting. The jokes he told or his humor was similar or identical to that of dozens of other preachers I have heard. Yet people still laughed at his jokes, still applauded and still got excited even if he was cookie punched from a dozen other preachers. A few weeks ago I heard another preacher who was also a *temonah*, he spoke from his heart which we all knew was his heart joined with God. He did not shout, tell jokes he only talked about the love of God and how he was satisfied to just know Him and His sacrifice on the cross. This was enough for him because that was all he really needed. He was in the likeness or the *temonah* of Jesus. It has been said the greatest form of flattery is when someone imitates you. Some preacher says; "Turn to your neighbor and say "Be blessed." He gets a big response and before long preachers all over the country are making their congregation talk to each other. Maybe imitating Christ will not draw the big crowds, but it will bring great *saba* or satisfaction. I will be satisfied to awake with His likeness not the likeness of Big Time Charlie Preacher.

CHAPTER 18

Stop Shining

JOB 9:7: "WHO COMMANDS the sun and it rises not and seals up the stars." I don't get to see the stars too much here. 3:15 AM is the wake up time for us and since the bells ring for Compline at 7:30 PM most of the retreatants are in bed by the time the stars come out, including me. But I did have the chance to catch the stars this morning at my 3:15 AM wake up hour. I was able to see the stars, hundreds of thousands of stars, more stars than I can see in the city and they were set off with the backdrop of the Kentucky hills. There are sure a lot of them. The Bible tells us in Job 9:7 that at God's command he can seal up the stars. The word in Hebrew for *seal* is *chatam* which means to *be locked up or stopped*. In this context it means to *stop shinning*. I have read books on Astronomy that told how many stars have burn out centuries ago, but their light was so bright and they were so far away that even centuries later we are still seeing their light.

God allows us to keep seeing the light of a burned out star just as he allows us to keep seeing the light of saints who have *burned out* years ago. D.L. Moody's light keeps shinning with the school that he built over 100 years ago that has never moved from its doctrinal position and is still training hundreds of future pastors, missionaries and Christian workers every year. George Mueller's light passed on to heaven over 100 years ago but his light still shines with the children homes that he started and the faith that built those homes. Even today many believers read and hear of the faith of George Mueller who never asked a penny from anyone to support his ministry to orphan and destitute children. He only went to prayer and trusted God to provide.

Christians today and in the future are and will continue to be encouraged and challenged by the example and light of the faith of George Mueller. The list is long of saints who have gone on to heaven, yet their light continues to burn brightly as an example to us all. Their light shines even after their physical life has ended, just as the light of many stars whose physical existence has ended, yet it still shines brightly in the sky.

My closing prayer as I begin yet another day of silence is that my light will continue to shine bright. It will continue to shine even after I join the others in that *great getting up morning*. It will continue to shine as an encouragement to the faith of others who continue their journey in this physical world.

CHAPTER 19

Ritual

I AM TOLD THAT the pretzel was invented by monks and the shape is the picture of ones arms, crossed and folded over their chest or heart in prayer. This was the posture I was encouraged to assume by the brothers during communion. As I am not Catholic I am not permitted to partake of the elements, but by folding my arms across my chest or heart in prayer, I am receiving the body and blood of Christ in my spirit which is, after all, the whole point and purpose of communion.

The brothers pause seven times a day to pray, although they are always in an attitude of contemplative prayer. During these seven periods of prayer throughout the day known as Vigils, Lauds, Terce, Sext, None, Vespers, and Compline they are praying from the Psalms. In this exercise they will go through all 150 Psalms every two weeks. Ok, you do that seven times a day, week after week, month after month, it can become a routine or a ritual. But then many Protestant Christians I know doggedly get up every morning and struggle through a half hour of quiet time. They try to perform at least a half hour of prayer and reading from the Word of God. Is that not a ritual? Some will put in a CD of Scripture being read and go about their business paying little attention to what is read. Children are encouraged to memorize Scripture in Sunday School for little prizes. They do not understand what they are memorizing, they just like getting the rewards. Is that not ritual?

Yet, when the chips are down and you do not have a Bible handy, how many times does a Scripture verse you don't even remember reading come back to you. Do not the Scriptures In Isaiah 55:11 teach that Gods Word will not return void? The word *void* in Hebrew is *reygam* which means to *be without any effect*. Does it not say in Hebrews 4:12 that His Word is sharper than any two edged sword? Someone can stand up and quote Shakespeare and I may not understand a word they say and I will end up getting bored or yawning. If I get into a tight spot I generally do not start quoting Shakespeare for comfort nor can I usually think of a good line from Shakespeare, but the Word of God comes very quickly to my mind and brings comfort and peace. When the brothers chant the Psalms, I have a hard time following what they are saying, but I know it is the Word of God and I am almost brought to tears just hearing the Word of God although I cannot really make out the exact portion of Scripture they are reciting.

The difference between Shakespeare and the Word of God is that there is the power and the very presence of God embedded in His Word. I can physically feel something when the Word of God is spoken. Cleansing and healing waves flow over me when the Word of God is spoken.

Much of what the brothers' practice is out of the scope of my personal religious persuasion, I am after all still a Baptist at heart. Yet, I cannot deny that there is a certain peace, serenity and contentment about the brothers. Oh, I know you will say it is their life style where they are free from the pressures and stresses of modern life. For the most part I would agree. Still, I cannot help but believe that a lot of that peace comes from being exposed continually to the power of the Word of God. The Word of God truly has a purifying effect on our hearts.

I remember reading a story in the Jewish Talmud about a student who complained of another student to his rabbi saying that this student only studied the Torah so he could become so knowledgeable that people will be impressed with his learning and say flattery things about him. The rabbi replied, "Don't worry, the Torah will purify his motives." I suppose reciting Scripture over and over can become a ritual, maybe playing a CD of Scripture being read is just ritual or it may even be done with mystical intent. Yet, there is something peaceful and joyful in listening to Scripture being read or spoken, even if you do no fully comprehend what you hear or are not even paying attention. Yet, our spirits are listening very intently. Later that day, week, month or even years we may find ourselves quoting a Scripture verse to ourself wondering from where that came. It came from our spirit that was intently listening when your flesh was preoccupied.

CHAPTER 20

Devekut

HAPPY BIRTHDAY TO ME. Fifty years ago on this date I was born again, it is my spiritual birthday. I did not plan to spend my golden anniversary with Jesus in silence, it just happened that way. I suppose it is just a coincidence. To use a good Pentecostal term maybe it is a God-incident. As someone once said, "It is funny how when I pray coincidences happen and when I stop praying coincidences stop happening." Nonetheless, being cloistered away in silence it is very unlikely that this birthday will be celebrated at Chuckie Cheese. It will be a time of reflection of fifty years of a growing relationship with the Jesus whom I have learned to dearly love. The joy I felt that day fifty years ago I still feel today, only it is somehow richer, purer, deeper and sweeter than it was fifty years ago. He has been my dearest friend down through the years. This old ship has been through many a storm in the last fifty years. It has been beaten and battered, it's mast is shredded, it's rudder is broken and it's haul is taking in water. But the Rock that I am anchored to, it still holds—that Rock still holds.

Another retreatant just walk by sobbing rather loudly. Hey, I thought we were to be silent? I guess the expressions of the heart are exempt from that rule. It is strange how the touch of God expresses itself in tears. In this environment no one seems to notice when someone is weeping, we all just callously pay it no mind or attention. It is sort of a God thing and He is better able to deal with it than us, besides what would we say? We are not allowed to speak.

I feel Jesus calling me to a devekut. Deuteronomy 13:4: "Ye shall walk after the LORD your God, and fear Him, and keep His commandments, and obey His voice, and ye shall serve Him, and cleave unto Him." That word *cleave* in Hebrew is *devekut* which is a very important word to the Orthodox Jew. It literally means to cling to God as He clings to you. It is like a child clinging to his mother or father out of pure love, not wanting to let go, to just stay in that parent's loving, protective and nurturing arms forever. It is like two lovers who go off to a secret place, shut out the world and just hold each other saying nothing, just finding joy and rest in each other's embrace. I render *devekut* as a hug. We are to fear Him, keep His commandments, obey His voice, serve Him and *hug* Him.

So, if you will excuse me, I feel God calling me to a secret, private place where He can give me my birthday hug. Of course, I shall hug Him in return and we will just spend a few hours holding each other, saying nothing, just enjoying each other's presence.

CHAPTER 21

Worship

PSALMS 29:2: "WORSHIP THE Lord in the beauty of His holiness." Many people have different ideas as to what worship is. To the brothers here at the Abbey, worship takes the form of liturgy and ceremony. To a Baptist worship is sitting for an hour in a church, singing a few *I like God* songs and listening to some dude who has been to Bible college and seminary tell us what the Word of God says. To a Pentecostal worship is hand clipping, dancing, raising your hands in the air and swinging from a chandelier. Actually, all of these things are not worship, just an expression or by product of worship. The word in Hebrew for worship is *shachah*. I have found this same word in other Semitic languages. Your lexicon will tell you it means to bow down or fall prostrate. But this word is more, oh so much more. The word is spelled Shin, Chet, and Hei. The Shin tells us that in worship God encompasses us with His passionate love. The Chet expresses the idea that in worship God uses His passionate love to bridge the gap between Him and us so that He can surround us with His Hei, His presence. Actually, when you look at the Hebraic origins of this word worship it is more passive on our part and more active on God's end. He really does all the work in worship. Somehow we get the idea that we have to dance, shout and sing to get God's presence. But as I said earlier, these are just the byproducts or the results of worship. Worship is simply giving yourself to God, one hundred percent. Worship is standing, sitting, bowing, or falling prostrate before God and saying: "I am yours, find whatever pleasure you can in me. In return we are filled with such joy over knowing that the God we love has found pleasure in us. We are awed that we can actually have such worth that the God of the universe actually wants and can draw pleasure from little old unworthy us. Such an experience only causes us to *whoop* for joy and swing from the rafters.

Shachah (worship) has its roots in a Ugaritic word. I remember translating a Ugaritic poem where a goddess name Anat falls in love with a mortal man and descends to earth to find pleasure in an intimacy with this human creature. Now think about this, the real joy of intimacy with someone you deeply love, such as your spouse, comes from being able to bring pleasure to that person. If you use your spouse to only bring pleasure to yourself then you have reduced your spouse to level of a prostitute. If you use worship to God to only bring pleasure to yourself, then you have reduced God to the level of a whore. If you use God to only bring you prosperity and comfort then you have not made Him a husband you are only using Him like a sugar daddy. God created a man and a woman to be a husband and wife. He created the marriage relationship to teach us about our relationship with God. In a marriage relationship the true joy of intimacy is when you bring pleasure to your spouse. Of course, if that is also your spouse's intention for you, then you will also receive pleasure in return. This creates a sort of an O'Henry's *Gift of the Magi* where the gift turns out to be totally irrelevant in light of the love behind it. That is *shachah, that is worship.*

This whole week that I have spent in silence I have not sung one praise song, attended one worship service with a worship team, guitars, drums etc. I have not danced or shouted (forbidden) or swung from the rafters (definitely not in that two story high chapel). But I did worship God. In fact my whole time in silence has been a time of worship as I have just allowed God to take pleasure in me. I let Him have me all to himself with no distractions. Can you dig it? Me! Sinful, flawed piece of humanity me and somehow the God of the universe has managed to find pleasure in an old slob like me. I just have to tell you, wonders never cease. You want a miracle, there is one right there, that this all powerful, all knowing God would take pleasure in the likes of me. I mean, you would think He could do better, you know maybe like Billy Graham? Yet, He created me so He will just have to take what He created.

One of the brothers is a potter. I watched him *pot* or whatever you call it. He must have built that lump of clay into a vessel a dozen times and each time felt there was some flaw, something that just did not fit his standard and so he ended up smashing it down back to a lump of clay before finally raising it up to the vessel he wanted. God spoke to me as I watch this and you can easily guess what He was telling me. I am nothing more than a lump of clay that He has to keep building up and smashing down back into a lump of clay every time He finds a flaw. He has to keep doing this until I am that perfect vessel that he longs to possess.

I know people will ask: "Well, what did God do for you in your week of silence, what did you get from God?" I am afraid I will have to reply that I got nothing. God got all the pleasure in having me all to himself for a week. However, in return, I found great joy in just bringing the one I love this joy.

I remember when I worked in an office. On everyone's birthday the office manager would take a collection to purchase some donuts or a cake for the person's birthday. Somehow one of the supervisor's birthday was overlooked. The next day he came to the office with a big box of donuts. I asked him what the occasion was and he said he purchased it for us, a gift to us for his birthday. Well, seeing today is my spiritual birthday, I am purchasing the donuts.

Chapter 22

Pleasurable Love

Song of Solomon 7:7: "How fair and how pleasant art thou. O Love, for delights." Oh, come now King James you can be more romantic than that. The words *pleasant art thou, O love* is one compound word *na'amethe'ahavah*. It is eight letters long in the Hebrew, which is a long word for the Classical Hebrew. It is the word *n'ameth'a (pleasurable) and ahavah (feminine love)*. Literally, what Solomon is saying is "your love is such a pleasure." This is how God speaks to us, when we love Him. Our love is such a pleasure to Him. Just the mere act of loving him brings him *n'ametha*. This is a pleasure that comes when feasting on some delicacy. We call it comfort food, it is a chocolate cake, ice cream, something which you would rarely allow yourself to indulge, but when you do, you savor every bite. Someone who has been on a diet knows *n'ametha* very well. To just bite into one piece of chocolate brings you into a land of pleasure, comfort, and you experience a euphoric feeling throughout your body. Just simply loving God brings Him this type of pleasure.

The words *for delights* is another long word in Hebrew, it also has eight letters buried in plurals, prepositions and articles. The root word is *'anak*, which is something so fragile, so delicate that you want to cuddle it, coo to it and protect it. It is something like a little puppy whose sad little eyes makes you want to reach out to hold it, kiss it and protect it. It is like a bride who has made herself completely vulnerable to her bridegroom such that he wants to wrap his arms around her, cuddle her, whisper sweet words of love to her, and protect her from any storm, danger or even insult. That is what it means when God says that He delights in us. That is *na'amethe'ahavah* which I call a *pleasurable love*.

CHAPTER 23

Desire

SONG OF SOLOMON 7:11: "I am my beloved and his desire is toward me. I am convinced this was translated by some grumpy old scholar sitting on his self-contained academic tower who hasn't kiss his wife in 20 years. What we need are poets, people like Elizabeth Barrett Browning involved in some of our translations.

"I am my beloved?" Really? Is that the best a translator can do? I mean they totally ignores the preposition Lamed. It should really say: "I am for my beloved." That is to say: "I belong to my beloved." Beloved in Hebrew here is *dodi*. This word has the idea of two people holding hands. The ancients believed that your heart was in the palm of your right hand. When you shook hands in those days it meant you were sharing your heart with that person. So Solomon's beloved was actually saying that her heart belongs to him, her lover.

But she also adds that his desire is toward her. The word for *toward* is '*al* which really means *over her*.

His desire for her hangs over her head and follows her around wherever she goes. To say it is his *desire* that hangs over her is putting it mildly. The word *desire* is *shug* which is a desperate desire, a longing or a craving, and even an addiction. This desire is so powerful you can actually feel it emanating from someone. The little peasant woman that Solomon loved actually felt his desire for her, it was like a cloud hanging over her head.

Could God actually have such a desire for us? Could He actually have a desire so strong that we could feel it? After spending my days in silence I can only say "Yes." In silence I could feel that nudge toward the Jesus that I love. I could feel his overwhelming desire to just let me put my head on His shoulder, to weep out all those years of pain and heartbreak, to share my years of disappointment, failures and then to hear Him gently whisper: "It's ok." And you know what? When He says it is ok, it really is ok. To have come through all those years and still have the same faith I had fifty years ago, that alone makes it all ok. It is all behind me and what is ahead is a day when I will see Him face to face.

As I conclude my week of silence and pack my bags to walk back to my car and leave this place of solitude to return to a noisy, confusing world I wonder what I will say when people ask: "Well, how was it?" What can I tell them? I had no vision of heaven, I did not see any pearly gates, streets of gold, or mansions, but in silence I have learned what heaven is like and it is glorious. In silence I have found a place that is filled with His love, His passion, His overwhelming desire and longing to give me a real long, never ending devekut (hug).

Oral tradition has a story of the prodigal son. Jesus, as a good rabbi, retold the story so familiar to his disciples, a story their mothers would tell them at bed time. Only in the story Jesus told the father just does not say to his son who ran away from home: "Come toward home as far as you can and I will meet you." In the way Jesus told the story the father runs down the road toward his son filled with *shug (longing)*. Reaching his wayward son he throws his arms around him, hugs him and kisses him. In the last few days I have met such a Jesus, I have felt his arms around me, I have experience His embrace and His *devekut (hug)*. I can now truly say that this is the reason God called me to silence.

Jesus and I had a final time together in that meditation room. He again asked me what I wanted. I thought of my request that first day for a powerful ministry. I was convinced that I was asking for something that came from the very heart of God. Now I realize what His heart is asking for and I tell Him the thing I want most is for Him to just have my heart and find whatever pleasure he can have with it. I told Him that in return He just keeps on hugging me and allowing me to keep entering into a devekut.

Whatever time I have left here on earth I only want to be allowed to enter His quiet room, His weeping room and be permitted to see the hearts that He is holding in His nail pierced hands. Those hearts that He weeps over. I want to weep with Him and if it is at all possible to find these heart's owners and let them know that there is a God weeping for them and that He wishes to build a Chet, a bridge, between their broken heart and His heart of healing.

Epilogue

It has been almost six months since my silent retreat and I am still experiencing new depths into the heart of God. As I sit on my porch a little bird has landed nearby and is just looking at me, chirping and dancing. I think of the Hebrew word for *bird* which is *siphar* and in its ancient form it is a reference to a bird singing and dancing. The word *siphar* is spelled Sade, Pei and Resh. The sages used to teach the Sade represents honesty, righteousness and purity. Indeed my little feathered friend has a pure heart as he sings his song. Yet if I were to listen to him with a pure heart, made righteous through the shed blood of Jesus, I will hear him speak. The next letter is the Pei which represents speaking. What is my little friend telling me in his song and dance, he is telling me of the last letter to his name, the Resh which speaks of the presence of the Holy Spirit.

My new friend has flown here to remind me that even after six months, hundreds of miles away from the quiet, hidden Abbey the Spirit of God is still just as real and present as he was in my time of silence. Yes, even sitting here in this noisy, confused city, the Spirit of God is just as real and precious as he was when I was hidden away in my time of silence. Once again I weep, but now I weep out of pure joy in the presence of the Jesus that I have learned to love with all my heart.

OTHER BOOKS BY CHAIM BENTORAH

HEBREW WORD STUDY—A
HEBREW TEACHER'S SEARCH
FOR THE HEART OF GOD

HEBREW WORD STUDY—A HEBREW
TEACHER EXPLORES THE HEART OF GOD

BIBLICAL TRUTHS FROM
UNCLE OTTO'S FARM

THESE BOOKS ARE AVAILABLE
THROUGH AMAZON.COM
OR
www.chaimbentorah.com

Chaim Bentorah and Chaim Bentorah Ministries are available for weekend Hebrew classes, conferences and speaking engagement. Please visit us at www.chaimbentorah.com for contact information.